ROGER WILLIAMS

FOUNDER OF RHODE ISLAND

SPECIAL LIVES IN HISTORY THAT BECOME

Signature LIVES

ROGER
WILLIAMS
FOUNDER OF RHODE ISLAND

by Michael Burgan

Content Adviser: J. Stanley Lemons, Ph.D.,
Professor of History, Rhode Island College

Reading Adviser: Susan Kesselring, M.A.,
Literacy Educator, Rosemount–Apple Valley–
Eagan (Minnesota) School District

COMPASS POINT BOOKS  MINNEAPOLIS, MINNESOTA

Compass Point Books
3109 West 50th Street, #115
Minneapolis, MN 55410

Visit Compass Point Books on the Internet at *www.compasspointbooks.com*
or e-mail your request to *custserv@compasspointbooks.com*

Editor: Sue Vander Hook
Page Production: Noumenon Creative
Photo Researcher: Svetlana Zhurkin
Cartographer: XNR Productions, Inc.
Library Consultant: Kathleen Baxter

Art Director: Jaime Martens
Creative Director: Keith Griffin
Editorial Director: Carol Jones
Managing Editor: Catherine Neitge

Library of Congress Cataloging-in-Publication Data
Burgan, Michael
  Roger Williams: Founder of Rhode Island / by Michael Burgan.
    p. cm.—(Signature lives)
  Includes bibliographical references and index.
  ISBN 0-7565-1596-3 (hard cover)
  1. Roger Williams, 1603?-1683—Juvenile literature. 2. Puritans—
Rhode Island—Biography—Juvenile literature. 3. Baptists—Rhode
Island—Biography—Juvenile literature. 4. Separatists—Rhode Island—
Biography—Juvenile literature. 5. Pioneers—Rhode Island—Biography—
Juvenile literature. 6. Providence (R.I.)—History—17th Century—Juvenile
literature. 7. Rhode Island—History—Colonial period, ca. 1600-1775—
Juvenile literature. I. Title. II. Series.
  F82.W7B87 2006
  974.5'202092—dc22   2005025215

Signature Lives

COLONIAL AMERICA

As they arrived in North America, European colonists found an expansive land of potential riches and unlimited opportunities. Many left their homes in the Old World seeking religious and political freedom. Others sought the chance to build a better life for themselves. The effort to settle a vast new land was not easy, and the colonists faced struggles over land, religion, and freedoms. But despite the many conflicts, great cities emerged, new industries developed, and the foundation for a new type of government was laid. Meanwhile, Native Americans fought to keep their ancestral lands and traditions alive in a rapidly changing world that became as new to them as it was to the colonists.

Table of Contents

Chapter 1

RELIGIOUS AND POLITICAL REBEL

❧❧❧

Looking around, Roger Williams saw a roomful of angry faces. It was October 9, 1635, and he was standing before the General Court of Massachusetts Bay Colony. The magistrates declared:

> Mr. Roger Williams, one of the elders of the Church of Salem, hath broached [introduced] and divulged [revealed] divers new and dangerous opinions against the authority of magistrates.

This wasn't the first time Williams had faced the General Court. He had already been asked several times to stop spreading ideas that went against the leaders of the colony. They wanted him to admit he had made a mistake and to promise not to do it

Roger Williams, English-born clergyman and founder of Rhode Island

again. But Williams continued to speak out against the colony.

The church and government were tied together in Massachusetts Bay. Laws were based on Puritan principles, and the magistrates had a duty to make sure citizens lived according to them. Williams, however, believed the church should be separate from the government.

Magistrates who served as judges for the General Court shouldn't punish people for not attending church or not following the Puritan faith, he claimed. A minister himself, Williams argued that only God could punish people on religious matters. The leaders didn't agree. They believed strongly that religion was part of everyday life and governed all political and social actions between citizens. Citizens had a religious duty to obey the laws of the colony and follow Puritan teachings.

Williams had already angered officials of the colony by writing two letters. One was to all the churches in Massachusetts Bay, explaining his argument with the magistrates. The ministers of the churches, however, refused to read his letter to their congregations.

Williams had also written to members of his own church in Salem. Don't have anything to do with the other Puritan churches in Massachusetts, he told them, or else he would no longer be their minister.

John Winthrop, governor of Massachusetts Bay and a member of the General Court, responded to Williams' first letter. It is filled with "antichristian pollution," he wrote. The magistrates, however, gave Williams a chance to think about his harmful ideas and change his mind.

John Winthrop served 12 terms as governor of Massachusetts Bay Colony.

The leaders told him to talk with other ministers who would show him how his views threatened church teachings. Williams rejected their offer. Instead, he agreed to debate Thomas Hooker, a Puritan minister. Their words were not recorded, but in the end, Williams held firm to his beliefs.

Finally, the magistrates could not tolerate this rebel any longer. They concluded their declaration against him:

> *It is therefore ordered, that the said Mr. Williams shall depart out of this jurisdiction within six weeks.*

Williams didn't have much time to pack up his

Both John Winthrop (1588–1649) and Thomas Hooker (1586–1647) opposed Roger Williams' ideas. Yet both men were also friendly with him. Winthrop, governor of Massachusetts Bay for many years, corresponded often with Williams, and for a time, the two men were business partners. Williams wrote frequently to Winthrop's son, also named John (1606–1676), as well. Hooker later had his own disagreement with the Massachusetts Puritans, and in 1636, he led a group of settlers who founded a new colony in Hartford, Connecticut.

family and belongings and leave Massachusetts Bay. If he refused to leave, the magistrates promised to physically remove him from the colony.

The members of Williams' church only added to his troubles. Those who had once supported him now turned against him. They admitted they had been wrong to support someone who opposed the Massachusetts Bay Colony, its magistrates, and the churches in the colony.

Because Williams had been sick several times that year, the court agreed to let him stay in the colony through the winter, as long as he didn't spread his detested ideas. Williams obeyed the leaders, or so it appeared.

He no longer shared his ideas in public, but in the privacy of his home, he told visitors that the leaders of the colony were wrong— they should keep civil and religious affairs separate.

Word of his private meetings got back to Boston, where the General Court met, and the magistrates

*Church atten-
dance was an
important part
of colonial life.*

once again gathered to discuss the Williams issue. They ordered him to be arrested and put on a ship headed for England.

When Williams heard that colonial officials were after him, he quietly sneaked out of Massachusetts Bay Colony. In January 1636, in the middle of a snowy winter, he set out on foot across land owned by the Narragansett Indians.

Williams finally settled in Providence, which

_Roger Williams
secretly left
Massachusetts
Bay Colony in
January 1636._

would later become part of the colony of Rhode Island. The official policy of this new settlement would hold firmly to the belief that anyone could "peaceably worship God according to the dictates of his own conscience," or inner sense of what was right and wrong.

Roger Williams is remembered as the founder of Rhode Island—one of America's original 13 colonies. More importantly, he was one of the first Americans to support and encourage what is now one of the basic beliefs in the United States—the separation of church and state.

Williams also said the state should not favor one church over another. It also should not try to shape its citizens' religious beliefs, he stated. He believed that everyone—including non-Christians—should be allowed to believe and worship as they choose. ❧

2 CITY BOY

Chapter

⚬⌒⚬⚬

Roger Williams came to Massachusetts Bay Colony when he was about 28 years old. His childhood home was in London, England, where he was born in about 1603.

London was a major European city at that time, with close to 250,000 people. On the west side of the city was the neighborhood of Smithfield, where Roger was probably born, although there is no public record of his birth.

Roger was the second child of James and Alice Williams. Sydrach was Roger's older brother. Two more children, Robert and Catherine, would follow to eventually complete the Williams family. Roger's father, a tailor, sold cloth in his shop on Cow Lane in Smithfield.

Roger Williams grew up in Smithfield, a suburb of London, England.

The Williamses probably lived in rooms above or behind the shop. Roger's father made a good living from his business and was fortunate to own other property in the neighborhood, as well.

The year 1603 was an important time for the citizens of England. Their beloved Queen Elizabeth I died that year after a 45-year reign, and the people got a new king, James I. The king tried to deal with the country's religious problems, which had been going on for decades. Elizabeth had been able to maintain a reasonable level of religious peace. But religion was still a hotly debated issue in England. James hoped to keep peace among the different religious groups.

James I (1566–1625) became king of England in 1603.

The national church was the Church of England, also known as the Anglican Church. Queen Elizabeth's father, Henry VIII, had established the church in 1534 after a disagreement with the Roman Catholic Church. Under Henry, Catholicism was no longer the main religion of England, and the pope was no longer the head of the church. Henry became the head of England's new church, and he made the decisions.

The Church of England was a Protestant church. It rejected some of the fundamental traditions and beliefs of the Catholic Church and established many of its own practices and rituals.

For many years, some people had wanted the country to return to Catholicism. They wanted the pope to again be their spiritual leader. Others, referred to as radical Protestants, thought the Anglican Church was still too much like the Catholic Church and wanted changes and reforms from within. As an adult, Roger would become one of them.

For England, 1603 was a year filled with death. A disease known as the bubonic plague swept through London, killing one out of every six residents. People tried to fight off the disease by eating garlic and burning strong-smelling substances, such as leather. The germs that caused the disease were carried by fleas that lived on black rats—something the people of England did not know at the time. Thinking that other animals might be to blame for the plague, residents killed cats and dogs rather than the rats.

When Roger was growing up, religion was very important to most Europeans. Holidays, activities, and weekly schedules revolved around the church calendar. For Roger's family, religion was a central part of their lives. It would affect Roger for the rest of his life.

His home was not far from the Holy Church of St. Sepulchre, where his family regularly attended

*Many Puritans
and Separatists
followed the
teachings of
John Calvin
(1509–1564).*

services on Sundays and heard sermons by John Spenser, their respected minister. Spenser was a Calvinist— someone who followed the beliefs of the 16th-century French religious thinker John Calvin.

Many Calvinists in England were called Puritans because they wanted to purify, or cleanse, the Church of England by making it less like the Catholic Church. They insisted it should follow the teachings of Calvin.

Religion was not the only thing that filled Roger's childhood. Smithfield was an interesting place. It was the site of a grand annual event—the Bartholomew Fair—which had begun in the 12th century as a religious celebration. Now it was like a trade show, where merchants sold cloth, candles, glass, and leather goods.

For two days in August, people flocked to the fair to buy goods and feast on roasted pig, apples, and gingerbread. Children bought dolls, rattles, and other toys, while jugglers, singers, actors, and puppeteers entertained the crowds.

A lively scene at the Bartholomew Fair as spectators enjoy a play featuring the devil and an angel.

Education was also an important part of Roger's life. He studied at the school run by his church and at home with his father. He learned to read and write English but also studied Latin, the language used throughout Europe by educated, scholarly people. Roger seemed to have a talent for languages. He had some knowledge of French and would eventually learn to speak Dutch.

At some point, Roger learned how to write in shorthand, a system of special marks and symbols used to quickly jot down someone's spoken words. When he was about 14, he was hired as a clerk by Sir Edward Coke, one of England's most famous jurists. During court proceedings, Roger took shorthand, recording every word that was spoken.

Coke sometimes challenged King James himself in court. He disagreed with the king on political matters and eventually ended up in prison for daring to question the country's sovereign monarch. Roger learned a lot from Coke. By listening to him in court, Roger learned the art of debate, something he would use often when people questioned his own ideas.

Roger Williams attended school at the Charterhouse, a private boys' school in London.

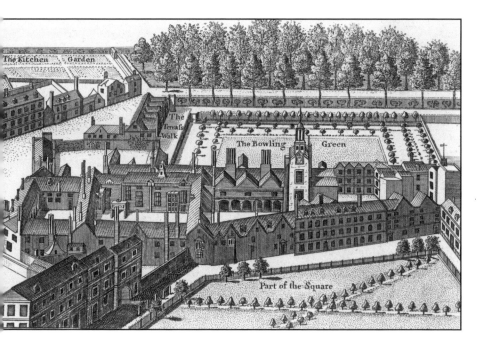

Roger respected Coke and called him his "much honored friend" who was "often pleased to call me his son." In 1621, Coke paid for Roger to enter the Charterhouse, a private school for boys.

Students at the Charterhouse began their day at 5 A.M. After morning prayers and Bible reading, instruction began. Roger studied Latin and Greek, practiced writing, and proved to be an excellent student. As a reward for two years of hard work and for having mastered his skills, Roger received money from the Charterhouse to continue his education. He would use it to attend Cambridge University, one of the top universities in England. ॐ

3 A Young Minister's Life

Cambridge in 1623 was a small town, much quieter than the crowded, buzzing streets of London. At the university, Williams studied at Pembroke Hall, where he lived with other students and the teachers.

He rose early and started the day with prayer. For the rest of the morning, students attended lectures or met privately with their teachers. In the afternoon, they attended more classes and studied. Everyone ate dinner together in the evening, while a student read aloud a selection from the Bible. By 9 P.M., students had to be in their rooms.

Williams continued his studies in Latin there. He read the works of great writers, practiced Greek, and learned about religion. His other classes included science, logic, and ethics—the study of right and wrong behavior. He also learned rhetoric, the skill of speaking well in public. Soon after arriving at the university, Williams won an award for his skill in languages and writing. The award usually went to students who planned to become ministers.

In 1627, Williams completed his studies and received his degree. In order to graduate, students had to sign a statement agreeing to accept the religious teachings of the Church of England. No one knows if Williams inwardly accepted all the Anglican teachings, but he did sign the statement. Then he remained at Cambridge to continue his studies for a higher degree.

Charles I became king of England when his father James I died in 1625.

When he was ready to receive his second degree, Williams was asked to sign another statement. By this time, however, it had changed. He now had to pledge his loyalty to the national church of England. Religion was changing in England. Charles I had become king of England in 1625, replacing his father, James, who had died that year. Charles' wife was Roman Catholic, and the new king began allowing elements of Catholicism into the Church of England. For his top religious adviser, he chose William Laud, who opposed Calvinist teachings and wanted the government to play a stronger role in religious affairs.

William Laud was a strong supporter of King Charles I.

Laud wanted churches to use government-approved prayer books and run their church services according to rules set by the government. Charles and Laud began cracking down on Puritans who refused to follow the rules of the Church of England.

In late 1628, Williams left Cambridge University without signing the statement and without receiving his degree. He traveled to Essex, just southeast of London, to begin his career as a minister. His first job was as a private chaplain for Sir William Masham, a Puritan and owner of a large estate. Nearby lived Masham's father-in-law, Sir Francis Barrington, and his wife, Lady Barrington. They were strong Puritans, as were many of their neighbors.

It was common for young men who wanted to become ministers to start their careers as private chaplains. Williams took care of the spiritual needs of everyone at the Masham estate, both family members and servants. He gave lectures on the Bible, held prayer sessions, and met with anyone who had questions about their faith.

Williams did have some free time, which he occasionally used for horseback rides to downtown London about 60 miles (96 kilometers) away. He happened to be there early in 1629, when Parliament and Charles argued over their roles in government. The angry king shut down Parliament and declared he would govern alone.

Disagreements in Parliament on March 2, 1629, led to the king shutting it down.

Williams also spent some of his free time thinking about marriage. In the spring of 1629, he wrote a letter to Lady Barrington, asking if he could marry her niece, Jane Whalley. The 26-year-old chaplain called himself unworthy and poor but added that he had received job offers that would boost his career. Lady Barrington disapproved of the marriage, however, and rejected his proposal.

Although Williams couldn't marry Whalley, he did find a bride before the end of the year. In December 1629, he married Mary Barnard, the daughter of a local minister. The two lived on the Masham estate for a little over a year. During that time, Williams thought about leaving England, where it was becoming more difficult for Puritans to worship as they wanted.

Puritans were finding that purifying the Church of England was very challenging. Since there was now no Parliament, they had nowhere to turn for help. Many of them started thinking about leaving England and sailing to the New World. A small group of Puritans led by John Endecott had already settled there in 1628 in a town called Salem. They had ties to the Massachusetts Bay Company, whose members and investors were mainly Puritans.

The Puritans still considered themselves members of the Church of England. But they believed that only people who publicly declared their faith in Jesus Christ as the Son of God should become members of a church congregation. The Anglican Church, on the other hand, automatically made every citizen a member of the church. Puritans also wanted to change the government. They said England should base its laws more closely on the Bible. That's what the Puritans were planning to do in the New World.

Endecott's Puritans were the first wave in a massive movement of Puritans who left England and went to Massachusetts. A large group of about 700 Puritans set sail in April 1630, under the leadership of John Winthrop. Williams didn't go with them, since he wasn't sure yet that he should leave England.

John Winthrop and hundreds of other Puritans came ashore at Salem, Massachusetts, in the summer of 1630.

He finally made up his mind when Laud clamped down even more on Puritans. Laud knew that chaplains of many wealthy Puritans were ignoring the rules of the Church of England. He began limiting their freedom, and Williams felt the pressure. Williams later wrote how Laud "pursued me out of this land." If he couldn't believe and preach as he wanted in England, Williams said, he would go to Massachusetts.

Williams' beliefs had changed by now. Instead of wanting to just purify and change the Anglican Church, he believed that people should separate from it. He was convinced that each church should be completely independent. Puritans who held this belief aligned themselves with the Separatists, a group that had been speaking up in England—and persecuted for it—since the late 1500s. Wanting to get rid of the national church was considered an attack on the English monarch and an offense often punishable by death. Williams would soon discover that his new Separatist beliefs would only bring him trouble. ॐ

> During the late 1620s, Puritans in Parliament battled King Charles and Bishop Laud over both politics and religion. The Puritan members of Parliament didn't like the changes Laud was making for the church. The lawmakers also didn't want to give Charles tax money he said he needed to fight foreign wars. Puritans Sir Francis Barrington and Sir William Masham were members of Parliament. Both briefly spent time in jail for opposing King Charles.

4 TROUBLE IN MASSACHUSETTS

❧⁓❧

On December 1, 1630, Roger and Mary Williams boarded the *Lyon*. The ship pulled out of Bristol, England, for a two-month voyage across the Atlantic Ocean. Joining the Williamses were about 20 other passengers. The ship also carried 200 tons (180 metric tons) of food and other supplies for Winthrop's group of settlers who had been in Massachusetts Bay Colony since July.

The winter crossing was not easy. The ship sailed through rough seas and cold winds. Passengers had little to do except pray and try to stay warm. During one storm, a passenger fell overboard, and the people onboard watched helplessly as he drowned.

When the *Lyon* finally arrived, the Puritans of Massachusetts Bay rejoiced. Their food supply was

Puritan settlers in Massachusetts Bay Colony

very low, and they had looked forward to the arrival of more provisions. They welcomed the wheat, peas, oatmeal, meat, and other goods that were unloaded from the ship. Winthrop noted in his journal, "Mr. Williams (a godly minister) with his wife" were among the new arrivals in Boston.

Williams soon received a job offer to be the assistant minister of the church in Boston. He stunned the Puritans, however, when he rejected the offer. He had met with the congregation and learned that the members still supported the Church of England. Williams later wrote that he could not work for "an unseparated people." His "conscience was persuaded against the national church and ceremonies." He didn't even want to become a member of the Boston church.

Roger Williams (c. 1603–1684)

Williams couldn't understand how Puritans could say that the Church of England was wrong and still keep ties to it. Williams thought it was more important to follow his conscience than to take the job, even though he had no other way to support himself and Mary.

Puritan leaders began to wonder if Williams was truly a godly person after all. Their concerns grew after he spoke out against the laws of Massachusetts Bay Colony. Puritan laws were taken from a part of the Bible called the Old Testament. The Ten Commandments, they said, were the basic laws God gave to Moses when he was leader of the nation of Israel, and should be the basis for their laws.

Williams claimed the first five commandments

Puritan laws were based on the Ten Command-ments, which they believed were given to Moses by God.

In 1608, a group of Separatists started leaving England for the Netherlands. The Dutch allowed them to worship as they pleased, but the Separatists did not feel comfortable in their new home. They thought they should truly separate from Europe and settle in North America. In 1620, these Separatists and others who had remained in England set sail on the Mayflower. Traveling with them were some settlers who did not share the Separatists' religious beliefs. Instead, they hoped to find wealth in their new home. Today, the Separatists and the other settlers on the Mayflower are known as the Pilgrims. Their ship landed in Massachusetts, where they founded the colony of Plymouth.

were personal—they dealt with a person's relationship with God. The government should only pass laws that concerned relationships between people. They should punish thieves and murderers, not someone who doesn't want to go to church. Williams' beliefs were not popular with colonial leaders.

Soon after turning down the Boston job, Williams accepted a similar position in Salem. Although still part of Massachusetts Bay, the church members there were more open to Separatist thinking.

Officials in Boston were upset when they heard the Salem church had hired Williams. They wrote to John Endecott, leader of the Salem Puritans, and asked him if the Salem congregation really wanted a radical like Williams working there. No one is sure why, but in August 1631, after a stay of less than a year, Roger and Mary Williams left Salem and settled in the nearby colony of Plymouth Plantation.

Plymouth had been a colony

Roger Williams' church in Salem, Massachusetts Bay Colony

for 10 years when Williams arrived. Several hundred people lived there, including Separatists who had created a church with no ties to the Church of England. That church hired Williams as their assistant minister.

William Bradford, governor of Plymouth, noted that Williams' "teaching [was] well approved." Williams wasn't paid for his position, so he had to farm and trade with the Indians to make a living. He wrote, "[I worked] hard at the hoe for my bread."

In Plymouth, everyone raised their own food,

even if they had other jobs. If they were fortunate enough to grow more than they needed, they traded the excess with others.

Sometimes Williams did business with the Algonquian Indians in the area. He also took time to learn one of the Algonquian languages so he could tell them about his faith in God. Unlike most English colonists, Williams had a good relationship with the Indians and treated them as friends. Most colonists feared them and their non-Christian beliefs.

Williams had stronger Separatist beliefs than most residents of Plymouth. When some Separatists returned to England for a visit, they attended services in Anglican churches. Williams thought the separation had to be total at all times and that people should not go to the Church of England. Bradford wrote that Williams became "very unsettled in judgment" and "began to fall into some strange opinions."

By the summer of 1633, Williams no longer felt comfortable in Plymouth. He and Mary headed back to Salem, along with their first child, also named Mary, who had been born that year. Several people who agreed with Williams also moved to Salem, where he still had friends from his brief stay in 1631.

Throughout his life, Williams always won supporters, even as he preached ideas that most people disliked. His deep conviction that his views were right appealed to some people who were willing

William Bradford (1590–1657) was governor of Plymouth Colony.

to question the common beliefs of the day.

In Salem, Williams was once again under the watchful eye of the magistrates. They had heard about a short book he had written just before leaving Plymouth. In December, Governor Winthrop and his assistants read the book. They were shocked by Williams' statements, which said that English rulers didn't have the right to claim land in North America and then give it to settlers.

Williams believed that land in the New World belonged to the Indians. The English could claim it, he said, only if the Indians chose to sell it. He was particularly upset that the kings of England had claimed they could take the land and then give it away as a right from God. Williams didn't believe they had that right.

Winthrop and other members of the General Court demanded that Williams take back what he had written and swear his loyalty to the king. Winthrop wrote in his journal that Williams agreed to do that and to offer "his book or any part of it to be burnt."

Williams claimed he intended the book to be private, written only to Bradford. He didn't want to upset the magistrates, who were afraid

English colonists needed a patent to claim land and do business overseas. A patent was a legal document from a king or queen that granted people the right to use land that belonged to the government. King Charles I issued a patent for the investors who settled in Massachusetts Bay. But Roger Williams, in a book he wrote in 1633, suggested that the patent was illegal, since English rulers couldn't give away land that didn't belong to them. Winthrop and other leaders of Massachusetts Bay Colony didn't like any argument that suggested that their claim to the land they now controlled was not legal.

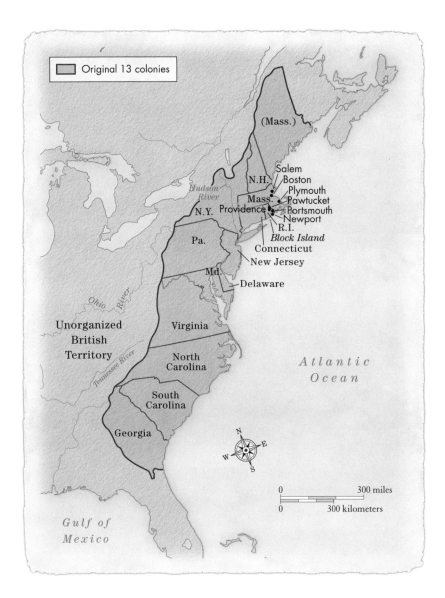

Legend: Original 13 colonies

(Mass.)

Salem
N.H. Boston
Plymouth
Mass. Pawtucket
Hudson
River
Providence Portsmouth
N.Y. Newport
R.I.
Block Island
Connecticut
New Jersey
Md.
Delaware

Pa.

Ohio River

Unorganized
British
Territory

Virginia

North
Carolina

Tennessee River

South
Carolina

Georgia

Atlantic
Ocean

Gulf of
Mexico

0 — 300 miles
0 — 300 kilometers

King Charles might cancel the colonial charter.

For now, Williams had avoided trouble, but he would not evade it for long. ❧

Thirteen colonies were settled on land that traditionally belonged to Native Americans.

Chapter

5 BANISHED

᠋ᦉ◦᠍◦ᦉ

In March 1634, Williams was involved in another conflict. Some Salem residents insisted that women should cover their heads during church services, and Williams agreed with them. Other ministers in Massachusetts Bay said that women did not have to cover their heads. The issue was a small one, but to some of Williams' critics, it was another sign of his refusal to get along with others.

Later that year, another controversy arose. A new design of the English flag was introduced. It had a large red cross on it—which to some Salem residents appeared linked to the pope, the leader of the Roman Catholic Church. Some also thought that displaying a cross was like having an idol. Most Puritans rejected anything that related to Catholics or idols.

John Endecott, governor of Salem, publicly cut the controversial cross out of the English flag.

John Endecott was so upset with the flag, called the "king's standard," that he publicly cut the cross out of it. For that, he had to appear before the General Court. There was no proof that Williams was involved with the flag cutting, but most believed he was. The Puritans regarded the flag as unspiritual and refused to use it in New England until the 1690s.

In the fall of 1634, the minister of the Salem church died, and Williams became its unofficial spiritual leader. Later, he was named official minister of the church. His Separatist views appealed to some church members. The women of the congregation were happy that Williams let them speak during church services, something that most churches refused to do.

Meanwhile, Williams questioned England's claim to Massachusetts land once again. He wrote a letter to King Charles on the subject, although he never sent it. Williams said it was evil for the king to give away land he didn't own. In March 1635, when the General Court heard about this, he was ordered to appear. He was told to stop spreading these beliefs, and sent home.

Williams had to appear before the court again on April 30. This time, the magistrates were angry about his views on a new oath all male residents had to take. By taking the oath, men promised to be loyal to the governor of Massachusetts Bay and the colony's other elected officials. The oath ended with the words "so help me God." Williams claimed it was wrong to have men who were not members of the church promise to do something in God's name. This lumped true Christians with "a wicked man in the worship of God," he said. He wanted church affairs and civil affairs kept separate. In fact, he didn't think anyone should take an oath or swear anything in God's name. At the request of the General Court, other Puritan

The sound of a drum meant that church was about to begin.

ministers debated the issue with Williams, but he would not change his opinion.

Williams continued to speak out about separating church and civil affairs. He repeated that the magistrates could not pass laws based on the first five commandments. In July, the General Court once again demanded that Williams come to Boston. He had about two months to prepare for his appearance. During that time, John Cotton, a respected Boston minister, wrote letters to Williams. Cotton hoped to convince him to change his mind. As always, Williams stuck to his beliefs.

John Cotton (1584–1652) was opposed to Roger Williams' beliefs.

Williams' conflicts with the magistrates also involved other issues. Residents of Salem claimed they owned land in what is now Marblehead. They needed the General Court's permission to take control of the area. For a time, the court ignored the issue in order to punish the citizens for choosing Williams as their minister. Then in July 1635, the magistrates officially rejected the request for the land.

In response, Williams and the Salem congregation wrote a letter, calling on the Puritan churches of Massachusetts Bay to condemn the magistrates for using this issue as a punishment.

In Boston, church officials refused to read the letter to members of the church. Williams and a Salem resident named Samuel Sharpe wrote another letter. In it, they attacked Boston church officials for refusing to read the letter. Leaders of the church replied that they didn't want to get involved in a civil affair. Williams and Sharpe said the issue was religious, not political, because of the magistrates' "disobedience against the Lord Jesus."

As trouble swirled around Williams, he lost support in the Salem congregation. Some even rejected his Separatist beliefs. In August, Williams wrote to the congregation, stating he would leave the Salem church if the members did not agree to break away from the other Puritan churches of

Roger Williams first met John Cotton in England. Cotton arrived in Massachusetts Bay in 1633 and immediately became the most respected minister in the colony. Cotton often debated Williams on his religious beliefs, and later the two men wrote each other long letters. Although Williams rejected many of Cotton's religious ideas, he truly honored Cotton. Other respected Massachusetts ministers were part of Cotton's family. His daughter Maria married Increase Mather, and they had a son named Cotton. Father and son, both ministers, wrote often on religion and played key roles in the Salem witch trials of 1692.

Massachusetts Bay. The congregation refused to do what he asked.

On October 8 and 9, 1635, Williams made his last appearances before the General Court. The magistrates and ministers of Massachusetts Bay reached a final decision. Williams' words and actions posed a dangerous threat to the colony's civil and religious order, they declared. He had to leave Massachusetts Bay forever.

Williams was able to delay his banishment for about three months by claiming he was sick. Now, however, the magistrates were tired of waiting for him to leave. They were also upset that he was still challenging Puritan ideas and talking about separation of church and state.

Winthrop wrote about what the General Court had learned about Williams:

> *[Williams] had drawn above 20 persons to his opinion and they were intended to erect a plantation about the Narragansett Bay.*

Puritan magistrates were concerned about this new settlement on the Massachusetts Bay border. They were worried that Williams and his followers would spread a Separatist religious infection, as they called it.

In January 1636, Captain Thomas Underhill

Roger Williams says goodbye to his family before leaving Massachusetts Bay Colony.

arrived at Roger Williams' home in Salem. His mission was to take Williams to Boston and place him on a ship headed for England.

Friends had warned Williams about the plan to send him back to England. When Underhill arrived, Williams was gone. ✍

6 INTO THE WILDERNESS

Chapter

❧⚶❧

A few days before Underhill's visit in January 1636, Williams had quietly slipped out of Salem and headed south. His destination was the Indian lands west of Plymouth. Williams later wrote, "My soul's desire was to do the natives good and to that end learn their language."

For weeks, he was exposed to the snowy wilderness. Still, he trudged on and was finally found by the Wampanoag Indians, who took him to the winter village of Massasoit, their sachem, or chief. Massasoit agreed to sell Williams some land next to the Seekonk River so he could start a plantation.

Soon, Williams was joined by several men from Salem and nearby Dorchester. One of them was Williams' family servant, Thomas Angell. The other

The Indians helped Roger Williams and sold him some of their land.

men had either been banished from Massachusetts or were poor and looking for a chance to find wealth. Williams was not particularly friendly with the men, but he let them join him anyway. The men had brought tools, food, and seeds with them. In the spring, the men helped Williams build simple huts on his newly purchased land.

As they were planting seeds, a message arrived from Edward Winslow, now the governor of Plymouth and a good friend of Williams. Winslow "lovingly advised me … to remove but to the other side of the water," Williams later wrote. The governor was afraid the leaders of Massachusetts Bay would be angry that Williams was living so close to land claimed by Plymouth. If Williams moved to the other side of the Seekonk River, said Winslow, they would be far enough apart and still be "loving neighbors together." Despite the kind words, Williams realized that Plymouth now considered him an outcast, too.

Nevertheless, Williams and his followers took Winslow's advice and crossed the river. They met with Canonicus, one of the sachems of the Narragansett tribe. Williams bought land from them along the east bank of the Great Salt Cove, where the Mossasuck and Woonasquatucket rivers converge. He named his new settlement Providence. He and the other men quickly prepared the land for planting. Others from Salem began moving to Providence, and by the end of the year, about 30 people lived there.

Edward Winslow (1595–1655)

Williams now took on a new role—political leader. Since he owned the land, he decided how it would be divided. He joined with the heads of each household to make decisions on how to run the new village and create local laws. Williams was clear that laws should only deal with civil affairs and not religion. In 1637, the settlers officially made Providence a town.

To Christians, the word *providence* refers to special help or care sent from God. Because Roger Williams sensed God's merciful providence, he called his settlement Providence. At first, the town was called New Providence—perhaps so it would not be confused with another English settlement called Providence, founded in 1630 off the coast of Central America by Puritans. That settlement ended in 1641, after Spain conquered the island.

Some time later, Williams sent for his family. His wife arrived with their daughter, Mary, and the newest member of the family, a daughter named Freeborn. At first, Williams struggled to support his family. He was in debt often during his early years in Providence.

In the past, he had traded with the Indians for furs, which he sold in England. Now he put his efforts into building a home, planting crops, and creating a community. When Winslow visited Providence, he saw how poor Williams was and slipped a gold coin to his wife.

The Williams family probably lived as most New England settlers did at that time. For shelter, they had small wooden homes with a fireplace to cook their food and keep warm. Outside, they grazed cattle and raised corn and beans, which were common foods among the Wampanoag and Narragansett Indians. Settlers also grew crops they had raised in England, such as peas, carrots, and barley. Williams started several business ventures in Providence, set up a trading post, and bought a small island with John Winthrop.

Roger Williams built his house in Providence.

In letters to Winthrop, Williams wrote about his efforts to settle Providence. He discussed Indian affairs and in August 1636 told Winthrop that the "Pequots hear of your preparations." A war was brewing between the Pequot Indians and Massachusetts Bay Colony. The Narragansetts were also involved. The Pequots were being blamed for the deaths of two Massachusetts traders on Block Island, just south of Providence. Massachusetts Bay responded by sending troops to attack the Indians.

Officials in Massachusetts Bay feared that the two Indian tribes would unite in a war against the colonists. They needed Williams' help. Since he had good relations with the Narragansetts, they asked him to meet with Canonicus and Miantonomi, the tribe's two most important sachems. It was hoped Williams could convince the Narragansetts not to join with the Pequots.

That October, he met with the two Narragansett sachems. Pequot leaders met with them at the same time. Williams felt uneasy around the Pequots, who were known as fierce warriors. He thought their "hands and arms … reeked with the blood of my countrymen murdered and massacred by them."

Williams' meeting with the Narragansett sachems was a success. When he asked them to sign a treaty of friendship with Massachusetts and not join the Pequots, they agreed. Tension grew, however, between the colonists and the Pequots. Early in 1637, the Pequots attacked several settlements in the Connecticut colony. With the help of the Mohegans, a Connecticut tribe, Massachusetts Bay and Connecticut responded by sending troops to the main Pequot village near Mystic River.

In April, Williams met again with Canonicus and Miantonomi to convince them to honor their promise to help the colonists. Again, Williams was successful. A few weeks later, Narragansett warriors joined the colonists in their war against the Pequots and helped to defeat them in a major battle. Williams said the victory was "through the mercy of the most High"— God. Throughout the colonies, Puritans believed that

A Pequot village was destroyed by colonists in 1637.

God was the source of their greatest achievements. On the other hand, they viewed their sufferings as God's punishment for breaking His laws.

After the main battle with the Pequots, Williams wrote to Winthrop, telling him about the captives that were taken and his contact with the Indians. He also wrote a paper about his Separatist beliefs and his opinion that Indian captives should not be made permanent slaves. No matter what was going on in his life, Williams' relationship with God was in his thoughts and writings. He still worried about political and religious leaders preventing people from following their own principles. That issue would once again spark trouble in Massachusetts Bay Colony.

7 BUILDING A COLONY

Chapter

❧⟨✦⟩❧

Roger Williams was not the only religious radical in the colonies. In 1637, Anne Hutchinson also threatened the leadership of Massachusetts Bay Colony. She was one of several people who questioned the colony's Puritan beliefs. She agreed with the Puritan teaching that a person cannot earn salvation by doing good works. But she challenged the belief that people had to live a perfectly moral life after they were saved.

Puritan leaders argued that society would be stable and orderly if its citizens had to live a moral life. Besides, they claimed, what better way to tell if people were truly the elect—the chosen of God—than by their upright living? Hutchinson denied the connection between salvation and good behavior. She accused the leaders of preaching a covenant of works—that salvation depends on the good things a person does.

Many Puritans disagreed with Hutchinson and her followers. The argument was splitting the Boston church. The conflict carried over into politics. Henry Vane, the current governor of Massachusetts Bay Colony, supported Hutchinson's ideas. But Winthrop opposed them because of the conflicts they were creating in the church.

Anne Hutchinson (1591–1643)

In November 1637, the colony put Hutchinson on trial, accusing her of "promoting and divulging of those opinions that are the causes of this trouble." During her trial, Hutchinson declared that the Holy Spirit spoke directly to her. She also claimed that she could determine who was or was not saved. Then she announced there were only two ministers in the colony who were truly saved—John Cotton and John Wheelwright, pastor of the Puritan church at Mt. Wollaston.

Leaders of Massachusetts Bay took action. They banished Wheelwright from the colony for agreeing with Hutchinson and preaching radical ideas about the Holy Spirit. Authorities also cracked down on other Hutchinson followers and sympathizers, ordering many of them to leave the colony.

They went into exile at Narragansett Bay, where

Religious issues and other disagreements caused conflicts among colonists.

Williams helped them buy Aquidneck Island from the Narragansetts. There they started a settlement at Pocasset (later called Portsmouth) on the north end of the island. Hutchinson eventually joined them after spending the winter in prison in Boston. She was tried and banished from the colony as well as banned from her church.

On the island, Hutchinson's followers built two towns, Portsmouth and Newport. Later, the colonists called the area Rhode Island. But the religious conflicts weren't over for these rebels of the Puritan faith. Trouble was brewing around a Portsmouth resident named Samuel Gorton.

Gorton had already been banished from Plymouth for his radical religious beliefs. At first, he was welcome in Portsmouth, since he seemed to share Hutchinson's ideas. But some of Gorton's views were too extreme for the people there. He said that men and women were completely equal. He also believed the Holy Spirit was inside everyone, and people could choose not to obey civil laws. Finally, leaders of Portsmouth banished Gorton, and he moved to Providence.

Even Williams, who thought people should have the liberty to follow their conscience, had trouble with Gorton. In March 1641, he wrote to Winthrop that Gorton was "bewitching and bemaddening poor Providence. … All suck in his poison." Williams must have been relieved when Gorton and his followers moved out of Providence—until that move created even more political problems.

In 1642, Gorton settled in Pawtuxet. Some residents there, led by William Arnold, did not want Gorton near them, and they asked the leaders of Massachusetts Bay to help them get rid of him. They refused, since Arnold's group was not part of their colony. However, they said that if Pawtuxet became part of Massachusetts Bay, they would take action.

This worried Williams and many others in Providence. If Massachusetts Bay controlled nearby Pawtuxet, it might try to take their land, too, or become involved in their affairs.

In 1643, Williams' fears seemed to be coming true. Neighboring colonies formed a military alliance called the United Colonies of New England. Rhode Island was excluded from the agreement. Now

As Williams established what would become the colony of Rhode Island, he remained devoted to his faith. He still served as a minister and began holding religious services in his home. In 1638, his congregation became part of the first Baptist church in America. The Baptists, like the Separatists, were opposed to the Church of England. But unlike the Separatists, the Baptists did not believe in baptizing babies. Instead, they baptized adults, since they believed that only an adult could truly choose to accept Jesus Christ as the Son of God and understand his teachings. Williams did not remain a member of the Baptist church for long, but he always defended the rights of its members to worship as they chose.

Williams wanted officials in England to confirm that Rhode Island towns owned their land and had a right to govern as they wanted.

Leaders of the Rhode Island settlements wanted Williams to go to England and get an official charter from the king. That way, they could form their own government, and Massachusetts Bay would not be able to control their land. Williams made a hasty trip to London.

Boston was the nearest seaport, but Williams could not set sail there because of his banishment. Instead, he went to New Netherlands, which was later called New York.

On his voyage, Williams wrote *A Key Into the Language of America*. In the book, he explored the language and customs of the Indian tribes he knew so well.

When he arrived in England, the country was facing extremely difficult times. King Charles had successfully kept Parliament shut down throughout the 1630s. But an outbreak of war with a group of Calvinist rebels in Scotland forced Charles to ask for Parliament's help. He needed money for this new war,

A Key Into the Language of America offers some of the best descriptions of Indian life in New England during the 1600s. Williams described how the Indians farmed and fished, what their homes were like, and what they ate. He also noted how the Indians acted with him: "They are remarkably free and courteous, to invite all strangers into their houses ... and [I] have reaped kindness again from many." Williams said that the Indians treated the English much better than the English treated them.

A KEY into the

LANGUAGE

O F

AMERICA:

O R,

An help to the *Language* of the *Natives*
in that part of A M E R I C A, called
NEW-ENGLAND.

Together, with briefe *Observations* of the Cu-
ftomes, Manners and Worfhips, *&c.* of the
aforefaid *Natives*, in Peace and Warre,
in Life and Death.

On all which are added Spirituall *Observations*,
Generall and Particular by the *Authour*, of
chiefe and fpeciall ufe (upon all occafions,) to
all the *Englifh* Inhabiting thofe parts ;
yet pleafant and profitable to
the view of all men :

BY ROGER WILLIAMS
of *Providence* in *New-England.*

LONDON,
Printed by *Gregory Dexter*, 1643.

*Title page of
Williams' book,
published in
1643*

and he needed Parliament to raise taxes.

The king reinstated Parliament, and the lawmakers were called back to duty in London. Then members of Parliament confronted the king. They wanted him to change certain policies that persecuted the Puritans. They also wanted the king to allow Puritans to be more involved in government.

Parliament wanted an end to the civil war that had erupted just months before Williams arrived in London. The two sides were clearly divided. On one side were soldiers loyal to the king. On the other were the Puritans and others who opposed him. Charles, who feared he might be killed, fled London. Bishop Laud, the longtime enemy of the Puritans, was arrested and put in jail.

Charles I and his supporters stormed Bristol in 1643.

It was a time of crisis for England. Williams

wanted a charter, but English officials had more serious matters to worry about. Then Williams faced another obstacle. Massachusetts Bay had sent people to London to stop him from getting a charter.

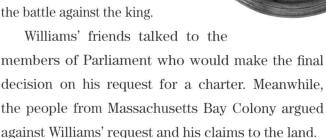

Now he turned to some of his powerful friends for help. He contacted Sir William Masham, who had given him his first job, and Oliver Cromwell, a Puritan leader in the battle against the king.

Oliver Cromwell ruled England as Lord Protector from 1653 to 1658.

Williams' friends talked to the members of Parliament who would make the final decision on his request for a charter. Meanwhile, the people from Massachusetts Bay Colony argued against Williams' request and his claims to the land.

By one vote, a committee within Parliament granted a charter to the "Incorporation of Providence Plantations in the Narragansett Bay in New England." It united Providence, Portsmouth, and Newport into one colony. Later, it would include Warwick, a town Samuel Gorton had founded at the end of 1642. Williams' trip to London was a success.

Before he left London, Williams wrote another

book—*The Bloudy Tenent of Persecution, for Cause of Conscience.* For the most part, the book was written to challenge John Cotton and his beliefs. It also addressed a religious debate going on in England over changes that some lawmakers wanted to make in the Church of England.

In the end, Parliament passed laws that required all English citizens to worship in the same way. Puritan standards were strictly enforced. Among other rules, there would be no dancing or card playing, and everyone would observe the Sabbath by reserving one day a week for worship. All churches in England had to follow the same set of standards.

Williams thought Parliament made a mistake by telling people how they had to worship. He said that power belongs to the people in a society. He spelled out his ideas in his book, which called for freedom of religion and a clear separation of church and state.

He wrote that the religious beliefs of magistrates should not affect how they enforce laws—claiming their "power, might, or authority, is not religious, Christian, ... but natural, human and civil." Any laws regarding religion were a form of persecution, he believed, and even non-Christians should have the right to worship as they chose. Few people at that time accepted his ideas, however.

The book was published in London in July 1644. It became the most famous book Williams ever wrote.

It also made him a hated man—on both sides of the Atlantic Ocean.

In Boston, John Cotton began preparing his own book to attack Williams' ideas. In London, Parliament

All churches in England were ruled by the government.

Colonists were overjoyed when Williams returned with a charter from the king of England.

reacted by ordering all copies of the book to be burned, stating that it discussed "the tolerating of all sorts of religion." Not all copies were burned, however. Williams' friends in England kept some, and Williams brought a few with him back to Providence when he returned that year.

Signature page of the charter for the colony of Rhode Island

On his return to America, Williams carried with him a letter from several members of Parliament to the leaders of Massachusetts Bay. It asked the Massachusetts Bay magistrates to end their ban on Williams. Although the magistrates refused, they let the ship he was on dock in Boston and gave him permission to cross Massachusetts so he could travel to Providence.

Once again, Williams set out on foot from Massachusetts Bay, as he had done when he was banished in 1636. This time, however, he was not alone. Friends from England had come with him, and boatloads of happy settlers greeted him as he crossed the Seekonk River. They were glad that Williams had returned with a charter from the king. Now they had great faith that their colony would survive. ℘

8 MORE BATTLES

Chapter

❧❧❧

Soon after returning to Providence in 1644, Williams was chosen chief officer of the new colony, a position he would hold for three years. At times, it was not easy to govern the colony. Residents of the four main towns still valued their independence and did not always act as a unit. It took the leaders of the towns until 1647 to finally accept the fact that the colony had just one government.

Representatives from each town served in the government. Williams worked with them to write laws for what was called the Providence Plantations in Narragansett Bay. It would later be called Rhode Island and Providence Plantations.

While trying to create an effective government, Williams also served as a diplomat, trying to keep

Roger Williams tries to talk the Narragansetts out of joining with the Pequots in the approaching war.

peaceful relations with neighboring Indian tribes. In 1645, the United Colonies of New England joined the Mohegan tribe in a war against the Narragansetts. This Narragansett-Mohegan war, as it was called, had been going on for two years. Williams' good friend, Miantonomi, sachem of the Narragansetts, had been

Chief Uncas of the Mohegan tribe defeated the Narragansetts in 1645.

killed in the fighting.

Now Williams convinced the Narragansetts to pay a fine imposed by the United Colonies and give up their claim to land previously owned by the Pequots. If the Narragansetts refused, the United Colonies planned to invade Rhode Island and slaughter them like they had the Pequots.

Williams was also tending to personal issues. Deeply in debt from his trip to England and needing to earn a living, he spent more time at his trading post. Mary and their children sometimes joined him. The couple now had six children— Mary, Freeborn, Providence, Mercy, Daniel, and Joseph.

Williams' small trading business was on the shore of a cove in Narragansett Bay called Wickford Point. He used a large canoe and several smaller boats to transport goods that he sold and traded. Indians came to his shop on the many trails that led there. They traded homemade baskets and animal furs and skins for pots, pans, utensils, needles, thread, cloth, tobacco, and more. Many also wanted whiskey, but Williams refused to sell alcohol to them.

Several years before he died, the Narragansett sachem Canonicus asked Roger Williams to attend his funeral. He wanted Williams to bring cloth from his trading post so the sachem's body could be wrapped in it. Canonicus died in 1647, and Williams followed his wishes. He later noted that "when the hearts of my countrymen and friends failed me, [God] stirred up the … heart of Canonicus to love me as his son to his last gasp."

He saw the harm heavy drinking had done to people in the communities.

In a good year, Williams earned about 100 English pounds—the equivalent of $20,000 today. As he traded with the Indians, Williams also told them about his Christian faith. His goal was "to prove unto them by reason, that the Bible is God's word."

For several years, Williams worked long hours at the trading post. At times, he lived with the Indians he traded with. By their campfires, he wrote a short book called *Experiments in Spiritual Life and Health*.

During that time, his wife was sick and started to doubt her faith in God. Williams tried to boost Mary's spirits, telling her that "the Lord loveth a cheerful giver … a cheerful prayer" and that people could find what they needed in the words of the Bible. In his book, Williams apologized to his wife for the time they had spent apart and told her how he cherished the memories of their times together.

In 1651, Williams faced another test. Once again, political issues sent him across the Atlantic Ocean. William Coddington from Newport was challenging the colony's charter. He had resented it from the beginning and didn't want Aquidneck Island under the charter any longer. Coddington sailed to England to ask for his own charter. There he managed to get a charter that made him governor for life of a

Williams encouraged his doubting wife with words from the Bible.

separate colony of Aquidneck Island, which included Portsmouth and Newport. Officials in Providence and Warwick asked Williams to go to London to defend the colony's charter. They wanted to prove that the original charter was the only one that applied in Rhode Island.

To pay for the trip, Williams sold his trading post

and some property he owned. He wrote a letter to Boston officials, asking for permission to sail from the Boston port. They agreed, as long as he promised not to talk about religious issues while he was there. Joining Williams on the trip was his close friend, John Clarke, of Newport. Clarke, a minister and doctor, was sent by Portsmouth and Newport to help get Coddington's charter revoked.

Williams and Clarke reached London in early 1652. Parliament was now firmly in control of the government. It had been three years since the lawmakers had gotten rid of the king, who had caused them so much trouble. He was beheaded in 1649. The Puritans, led by Oliver Cromwell, now dominated Parliament. Williams hoped his friends in Parliament would help him halt Coddington's efforts to split up the colony. He also wanted the original charter confirmed so Rhode Island's right to exist was clear.

During his stay in London, Williams published several books he had written in America. One of them—*The Bloudy Tenet Yet More Bloudy*—continued Williams' religious war of words with John Cotton. It also praised Parliament for showing tolerance to a wide range of religious beliefs.

But Williams still thought there was too much persecution, which he called a "notorious and common pirate" that attacks the "consciences of all

Parliament had Charles I beheaded in 1649.

men … of all religions."

Williams stayed in London for more than two years. In a letter to a friend, he said he missed Mary, but he didn't directly ask her to join him in England. "I tell her how joyful I should be of her with me," he wrote, yet he also thought it was up to her to "wait upon the Lord for direction" on whether or not to come. Williams worried about her facing "the dangers of the sea."

Mary did not come to England, and Williams finally returned to Providence in the summer of 1654.

Clarke stayed in England to continue looking after the colony's interests. He and Williams had been able to prove that Coddington's charter was not valid. However, they had not yet obtained a new charter for Rhode Island, which upset some of the colonists.

The year Williams returned, he was elected governor of Rhode Island and faced new problems. Leaders in Massachusetts Bay, Plymouth, and Connecticut all claimed they had a legal right to land in Rhode Island. Residents of Rhode Island were bickering about how the government should be run, and they joined in the argument over who had legal rights to the land.

A 1664 map of Providence shows how properties were divided among the original colonists.

These problems prompted Williams to write a letter to the people of Providence. In it, he claimed

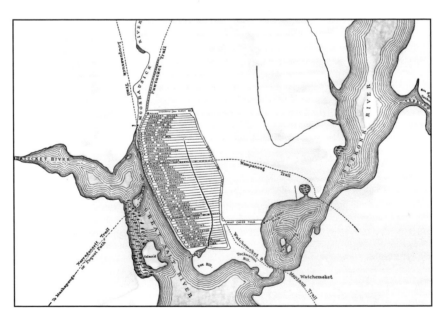

he was being blamed for many of the problems the colony faced. He had given up his time and his business to do what he could to keep Rhode Island safe. "I am like a man in great fog," he wrote, not knowing what he could do to make everyone happy.

Sometime in January 1655, another problem caused Williams to write yet another letter to the people of Providence. This so-called ship-of-state letter became one of his most famous writings. It was written in response to some residents who didn't want to be forced to serve in the local militia. The people argued that they should have the freedom to choose whether they served. It was a matter of conscience, they said. The leader of these protesters was Robert Williams—Roger's brother—who had arrived in Providence in 1644.

Roger answered his brother and the other protesters by comparing a community to a ship. The individual passengers had their own religious beliefs, he explained. "The liberty of conscience that ever I pleaded for," Williams said, was that no one should be forced to attend whatever church service the captain ordered. Likewise, the captain could not keep them from practicing their own faiths.

But Williams believed the captain—the government—had a right to keep civil order. The passengers—the citizens—had a duty to help protect the entire ship from troubles. Serving in the militia was one of those duties.

Under Williams' leadership, Rhode Island continued to be a colony that allowed religious liberty. In 1656, members of the Society of Friends led by George Fox arrived in the New World. These religious people, more commonly known as Quakers, tried to win converts to their faith.

The Puritans of Massachusetts Bay and the other Puritan colonies opposed their efforts and passed laws against the Quakers and their beliefs. Many were banished, but they found a home in Rhode Island. The colony's lawmakers said that Quakers "have their liberty amongst us, are entertained into

George Fox (1624–1690) wore his hat in church to show that he disagreed with the preacher.

our houses, or into any of our assemblies." Though Williams disagreed with the Quakers' religious beliefs, he accepted their right to believe and worship as they wanted.

Although Rhode Islanders were tolerant of others, they still disagreed with each other on certain issues. Williams was no longer governor after 1657, but he still found himself involved in disputes.

In the early 1660s, William Harris of Pawtuxet tried to claim land around Providence. Williams said that if Harris and his friends wanted land, they would have to buy it from the Indians. Harris argued that Providence had much more land than Williams claimed. But to Williams, it was a moral issue. He thought Harris was just being greedy and looking out for himself.

Williams wrote, "All experience tells us that public peace and love is better than abundance of corn and cattle." Despite his efforts, the battles over land continued for many years. ❧

9 FINAL STRUGGLES

Chapter

e◦x◦e

Williams was also still trying to resolve an ongoing issue with England. Oliver Cromwell had died, and a king once again ruled England. Charles II, son of the previous king, had taken over the throne in 1661. Puritans no longer ruled England.

John Clarke was still in London defending Rhode Island's interests and trying to get a new charter. Finally, after 11 years, his hard work paid off. In 1663, Rhode Island received a new royal charter signed by the king. Like the previous charter, it said that the colonists could worship as they chose. It called their liberty of conscience—or freedom to live according to their beliefs—a "lively experiment." Williams thought this liberty was the only way to keep order in a world where people held

A statue of Roger Williams in Providence honors the founder of Rhode Island.

such different religious beliefs.

The royal charter created a new type of government for Rhode Island. The people could now choose their own government leaders and make most of their own laws. Williams was chosen as one of 10 assistants to the governor, a position that he held until 1677. In the fall of 1664, he and the other magistrates started meeting twice a year with the lawmakers of the General Assembly.

Williams was involved in more than just colonial politics. He often visited Wickford Point and preached to anyone who would listen to his messages about God, Christ, and the Bible. At other times, he invited small groups of friends and neighbors into his home to talk about religious matters. What mattered most, he said, was a person's personal relationship with God. Though he felt that people should be able to worship as they pleased, he still tried to convince others to share his views. That desire led to a series of debates with the Quakers.

By the early 1670s, Rhode Island was home to many Quakers, who by now dominated the government. Williams detested their religious ideas. He thought they relied too much on emotion and didn't think reasonably about their beliefs. Quakers believed each person had what they called an inner light, or an inner voice, that told them what to do. Williams didn't accept this. He thought God spoke to

The Quakers were committed to the principles of peace, equality, honesty, and simple living.

people only through the Bible. He worried that the Quakers might disrupt society.

In 1672, Williams challenged George Fox, the founder of the Quakers, to a public debate. Williams wrote down some of his arguments. "The sufferings of the Quakers is no true evidence of the truth of their religion," he claimed. In addition, he said "their many books and writings are extremely poor [and] lame." Fox left Rhode Island before receiving Williams'

English-born Roger Williams migrated to Massachusetts Bay Colony but settled in Providence, Rhode Island, after he was exiled.

challenge, but three other Quakers agreed to debate him.

In August, Williams went by canoe from Providence to Newport—a distance of 30 miles (48 km)— where the debates would be held. Williams later wrote that God helped him and his "old bones" make the

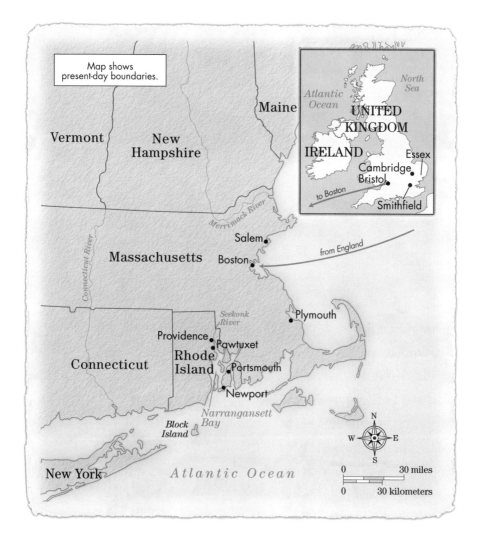

journey. He debated in Newport for three days. A crowd came to watch the debates, most of them Quakers. At times, the audience shouted out their opinions and disagreed. Someone called Williams an "old bitter man," but someone else was heard saying, "Methinks there is weight in Mr. Williams and his arguments." Williams focused on why he thought the Quakers were a danger to both Christianity and civil order. After the debates, he wrote down his arguments against the Quakers in a book called *George Fox Digg'd out of his Burrowes*.

Religious battles were not the only conflicts Williams faced in the 1670s. Troubles with the Indians once again led to a major war. The Wampanoags were peaceful while Massasoit was their sachem. But under his sons, Wamsutta and Metacomet, the tribe began to resent Plymouth, which continually took their land. The colonists often forced the Indians to sell their land to pay off their debts and the fines they had incurred for breaking

The Quakers first appeared in England during the 1650s. Their name reflected the belief that their bodies shook, or quaked, when touched by God's Spirit. The Quakers believed that Jesus died so that everyone had a chance to go to heaven, not just a few chosen by God. They also said a person could find God's grace through an inner light. This light was inside everyone, making everyone equal—an idea other Christians of the day did not accept. The Puritans passed laws outlawing the Quakers. Many Quakers ignored these laws and were jailed, banished, or killed. Between 1659 and 1661, four Quakers were hanged in Massachusetts Bay.

English laws. The colonists were also clearing and developing land that the Indians used as hunting grounds and farmland.

At the same time, Puritans from Massachusetts Bay were trying to convert the Wampanoags to Christianity. Tribal leaders feared that traditional Indian religious beliefs would die out if more of their people became Christians.

By 1671, Metacomet was the only leader of the Wampanoags. He was called King Philip, an English name he decided to use. His main village was in present-day Rhode Island in Bristol and Warren. Residents from Plymouth had recently established a new town named Swansea on the border of the Wampanoag lands. The Indians felt threatened by this nearby settlement.

In the spring of 1675, trouble broke out. Plymouth officials accused three Wampanoag Indians of killing a Christian Indian. The three were executed, and Metacomet's warriors responded by raiding the town of Swansea. The raid soon led to hostilities throughout New England that became known as King Philip's War.

Colonists from Connecticut, Massachusetts Bay, and Plymouth united to fight the Wampanoags. Soon, more Indian tribes joined the struggle. The Narragansetts entered the war after the United Colonies attacked their camp in southern Rhode

Island in December 1675. They took terrible revenge on the settlers and destroyed half the towns in New England. Many colonists were killed, but more native people lost their lives in the war.

Metacomet, leader of the Wampanoag Indians, came to be called King Philip.

In March 1676, the war came to Providence. As the Indians threatened the town, most of the residents fled to Aquidneck Island for safety. Williams was one of about 30 men who stayed behind to defend Providence. The Narragansetts burned down the town, including Williams' home. He told the attackers, "This house of mine now burning before mine eyes hath lodged kindly some thousands of you [Indians] these ten years." The Indians replied that Rhode Island was the friend of their enemies, Massachusetts Bay and Plymouth. The attackers moved on, but by the end of the summer, Metacomet had been killed. The settlers and their Indian allies (the Mohegans and Pequots) defeated the warring Indians in New England's worst Indian war.

Mary Williams had stayed in Newport during the Indian war. In August, she rejoined her husband. The residents of Providence were now starting to rebuild their town. Williams played an active role in this process, once again serving in local government. He also dealt with issues that affected all of Rhode Island. The colony was involved in border disputes with William Harris of Pawtuxet and its neighbors. The disputes with the other colonies—primarily Connecticut—would go on for many more years.

Williams was now about 73 years old, approaching the last years of his life and short on money. During King Philip's War, he had struggled financially and

Metacomet, also called Metacom, was killed by colonists in the summer of 1676.

had once asked the governor of Massachusetts Bay for money. In 1678, he received money and corn from Connecticut as a reward for treating its army with courtesy during the war. For a time, he and Mary turned to their son Daniel for financial support.

In the midst of his struggles, however, Williams' ideas on the separation of church and state didn't change. In a letter written in 1679, he said he had spent "40 years in a barbarous wilderness" trying to keep religion out of civil affairs and politics out of religion.

As was the style of debate in the 1600s, Williams had often used strong words against the people who disagreed. They had attacked him in the same way. Yet he thought he had always fairly considered his enemies' arguments. He once said he had tried to "present my thoughts in love, patience, and meekness."

By May 1682, when Williams was about 79, he referred to himself as "old and weak and bruised." Yet he still hoped to publish one more book, a collection of sermons he had preached to the Narragansetts. The sermons, however, were never published, and Williams died less than a year later, sometime in 1683. The exact date and cause of his death are not known.

Roger Williams was buried in Providence, but over the years, the exact location of his grave site was forgotten and has never been found. We may not know where he was buried, but what he did during his life will not be forgotten.

For several centuries, Williams has been honored as a man who always stood up for his beliefs, even when they were unpopular. He stood by the principle that people should be allowed to believe and worship how they choose.

Williams wasn't afraid to provide a safe haven

The Royal Charter of Rhode Island is in a vault outside the Senate chamber in the Rhode Island State Capitol.

in Rhode Island for people of all religious faiths. His efforts to keep religious issues separate from government have had a lasting effect on what later became the state of Rhode Island and the United States of America. ॐ

WILLIAMS' LIFE

c. 1603

Born in
Smithfield in
London, England

c. 1617

Hired as a
clerk by jurist
Sir Edward Coke

1610

1603

James I becomes
king of England
and Ireland

1608

Galileo constructs
the astronomical
telescope

1614

Pocahontas
marries
John Rolfe

WORLD EVENTS

1623

Attends Cambridge University

1621

Attends the Charterhouse, a private school for boys

1629

Hired by Sir William Masham as his private chaplain; marries Mary Barnard

1625

1620

The *Mayflower* with its Pilgrim passengers sails from England to North America

1628

John Bunyan, popular religious English author, is born

1624

England declares war on Spain

Life and Times

WILLIAMS' LIFE

1631

Arrives in Boston, Massachusetts, with his wife; moves to Salem; settles in Plymouth

1633

Writes his first book

1630

1632

King Charles I issues a charter for the colony of Maryland

1634

Jean Nicolet lands on Green Bay and explores Wisconsin

WORLD EVENTS

1636

Buys land from the Narragansett Indians and establishes the town of Providence

1635

Banished from Massachusetts Bay Colony

1637

Convinces the Narragansett Indians not to side with the Pequot Indians in a war with colonists

1640

1638

Louis XIV, future King of France, is born

1635

English High and Latin School, Boston, Massachusetts, oldest secondary school in North America, is founded

1636

Harvard College is founded at Cambridge, Massachusetts

WILLIAMS' LIFE

1644

Obtains a charter for Providence; publishes *The Bloudy Tenent of Persecution, for Cause of Conscience*

1643

Writes *A Key Into the Language of America*

1654

Elected governor of Rhode Island; reelected each year until 1657

1650

1642

Isaac Newton, English mathematician and philosopher, is born

1646

Blaise Pascal invents the syringe

1655

Christian Huggens discovers the rings of Saturn

WORLD EVENTS

1672

Holds a series
of debates
with the
Quakers

1676

Remains in
Providence during
King Philip's War

1683

Dies in
Providence,
Rhode Island

1680

1670

The Hudson's Bay
Company is founded

1681

The Canal du Midi,
a 150-mile (240-
km) long canal in
southern France, is
finished after eight
years of work

1682

The French
royal court
moves to
Versailles

DATE OF BIRTH: c. 1603

BIRTHPLACE: Smithfield in London, England

FATHER: James Williams (1562–1621)

MOTHER: Alice Pemberton Williams (1564–1634)

EDUCATION: St. Sepulchre church school; The Charterhouse; Cambridge University

SPOUSE: Mary Barnard (1609–1683?)

DATE OF MARRIAGE: 1629

CHILDREN: Mary (1633–1684)
Freeborn (1635–1710)
Providence (1638–1686)
Mercy (1640–1705)
Daniel (1641–1712)
Joseph (1643–1724)

DATE OF DEATH: 1683

PLACE OF BURIAL: Providence, Rhode Island

FURTHER READING

Allison, Amy. *Roger Williams: Founder of Rhode Island*. Philadelphia: Chelsea House Publishers, 2001.

Gaustad, Edwin S. *Roger Williams*. New York: Oxford University Press, 2005.

Kent, Deborah. *In Colonial New England*. New York: Benchmark Books, 2000.

Lace, William W. *Oliver Cromwell and the English Civil War in World History*. Berkeley Heights, N.J.: Enslow Publishers, 2003.

Slavicek, Louise Chipley. *Life Among the Puritans*. San Diego: Lucent Books, 2001.

LOOK FOR MORE SIGNATURE LIVES BOOKS ABOUT THIS ERA:

Lord Baltimore: *Founder of Maryland*
ISBN 0-7565-1592-0

Anne Hutchinson: *Puritan Protester*
ISBN 0-7565-1577-7

William Penn: *Founder of Pennsylvania*
ISBN 0-7565-1598-X

John Winthrop: *Colonial Governor of Massachusetts*
ISBN 0-7565-1591-2

ON THE WEB

For more information on *Roger Williams*, use FactHound.

1. Go to *www.facthound.com*
2. Type in a search word related to this book or this book ID: 0756515963
3. Click on the *Fetch It* button.

FactHound will fetch the best Web sites for you.

HISTORIC SITES

Roger Williams National Memorial
282 N. Main St.
Providence, RI 02903
401/521-7266
Park on the original settlement of Providence commemorates the life of Roger Williams

Roger Williams Landing Place Monument
Providence, RI 02906
401/785-9450
Where Roger Williams first stepped ashore in 1636 after being banished from Massachusetts Bay Colony

bishop
a church leader in charge of a city or area

chaplain
a member of the clergy assigned to an institution
or a family

charter
a formal document incorporating a colony, organi-
zation, or company

diplomat
person who represents a community or government in its foreign affairs

jurists
people having a thorough knowledge of the law

magistrates
government officials, such as judges, who carry
out the law

oath
a formal promise to do something, often naming
God as a witness

persecution
cruel and unfair treatment, often because of race
or religious beliefs

Puritan
member of a reform movement who wished to
purify the Church of England

radical
extreme compared to what most people think
or do

spiritual
relating to religious or sacred matters

Chapter 1

Page 9, line 5: "Today in History." *The Library of Congress: Memory Library.* 11 November 2005. http://memory.loc.gov/ammem/today/feb05.html.

Page 11, line 5: John Winthrop. *The Journal of John Winthrop, 1630-1649.* Abridged edition. Edited by Richard S. Dunn and Laetitia Yeandle. Cambridge, Mass.: The Belknap Press of Harvard University, 1996, p. 85.

Page 11, line 23: "Today in History."

Page 15, line 1: Raymond L. Camp. *Roger Williams, God's Apostle of Advocacy: Biography and Rhetoric.* Lewiston, N.Y.: The Edwin Mellen Press, 1989, p. 146.

Chapter 2

Page 23, line 1: Glenn W. LaFantasie, et al. *The Correspondence of Roger Williams*, Volume 1. Providence, R.I.: Brown University Press, 1988, p. 358.

Chapter 3

Page 31, line 9: *Roger Williams, God's Apostle of Advocacy: Biography and Rhetoric*, p. 105.

Chapter 4

Page 34, line 8: *The Journal of John Winthrop, 1630-1649*, p. 34.

Page 34, line 20: Edwin S. Gaustad. *Liberty of Conscience: Roger Williams in America.* Valley Forge, Pa.: Judson Press, 1999, p. 25.

Page 37, line 7: *The Annals of America*, Volume 1. Chicago: Encyclopaedia Brittanica, 1968, p. 81.

Page 37, line 10: Ola Elizabeth Winslow. *Master Roger Williams: A Biography.* New York: The MacMillan Company, 1957, p. 103.

Page 38, line 17: *The Annals of America*, Volume 1, pp. 81-82.

Page 40, line 23: *The Journal of John Winthrop, 1630-1649*, p. 62.

Chapter 5

Page 45, line 5: Ibid., p. 79.

Page 47, line 19: *The Correspondence of Roger Williams*, Volume 1, p. 27.

Page 48, line 18: *The Journal of John Winthrop, 1630-1649*, p. 87.

Chapter 6

Page 51, line 4: *Master Roger Williams: A Biography*, p. 128.

Page 52, line 10: *Liberty of Conscience: Roger Williams in America*, p. 48.

Page 55, line 4: *The Correspondence of Roger Williams*, Volume 1, p. 54.

Page 56, line 9: Glenn W. LaFantasie, et al. *The Correspondence of Roger Williams*, Volume 2. Providence, R.I.: Brown University Press, 1988, p. 611.

Page 56, line 27: *The Correspondence of Roger Williams*, Volume 1, p. 83.

Chapter 7

Page 60, line 20: Francis J. Bremer. *John Winthrop: America's Forgotten Founding Father*. New York: Oxford University Press, 2003, p. 297.

Page 62, line 27: *The Correspondence of Roger Williams*, Volume 1, p. 215.

Page 64, sidebar: *Collections of the Massachusetts Historical Society*, Volume III. Boston: Apollo Press, 1968. 21 Nov. 2005, http://capecodhistory.us/19th/MHS1794.htm.

Page 68, line 21: "The Root of American Religious Liberty—Roger Williams." 21 Nov. 2005, www.churchandstate.us/church-state/wm-cot1a.htm.

Page 70, line 2: *Master Roger Williams: A Biography*, p. 198.

Chapter 8

Page 75, sidebar: Ibid., p. 216.

Page 76, line 6: Ibid., p. 223.

Page 76, line 15: Ibid., p. 225.

Page 78, line 27: *Liberty of Conscience: Roger Williams in America*, p. 104.

Page 79, line 5: *The Correspondence of Roger Williams*, Volume 1, p. 367.

Page 81, line 4: *The Correspondence of Roger Williams*, Volume 2, p. 399.

Page 81, line 20: Ibid., p. 424.

Page 82, line 13: *Master Roger Williams: A Biography*, p. 258.

Page 83, line 17: *The Correspondence of Roger Williams*, Volume 2, p. 526.

Chapter 9

Page 85, line 13: Sydney V. James. *Colonial Rhode Island: A History*. New York: Scribner, 1975, p. 377.

Page 87, line 5: *The Correspondence of Roger Williams*, Volume 2, p. 648.

Page 89, line 6: *Roger Williams, God's Apostle of Advocacy: Biography and Rhetoric*, p. 174.

Page 92, line 7: *The Correspondence of Roger Williams*, Volume 2, p. 722.

Page 94, line 1: Ibid., p. 769.

Page 94, line 8: Ibid.

Page 94, line 11: Ibid., p. 777.

The Annals of America (Vol. 1). Chicago: Encyclopaedia Britannica, 1968.

Bremer, Francis J. *John Winthrop: America's Forgotten Founding Father*. New York: Oxford University Press, 2003.

Camp, L. Raymond. *Roger Williams, God's Apostle of Advocacy: Biography and Rhetoric*. Lewiston, N.Y.: Edwin Mellen Press, 1989.

Davies, Norman. *The Isles: A History*. New York: Oxford University Press, 1999.

Faragher, John Mack. *The Encyclopedia of Colonial and Revolutionary America*. New York: Da Capo Press, 1996.

Gaustad, Edwin S. *Liberty of Conscience: Roger Williams in America*. Valley Forge, Pa.: Judson Press, 1999.

James, Sydney V. *Colonial Rhode Island: A History*. New York: Scribner, 1975.

LaFantasie, Glenn W., et al. *The Correspondence of Roger Williams*. 2 vols. Providence, R.I.: Brown University Press, 1988.

Miller, Perry. *Roger Williams: His Contribution to the American Tradition*. New York: Atheneum, 1970.

Winslow, Ola Elizabeth. *Master Roger Williams: A Biography*. New York: MacMillan Company, 1957.

Winthrop, John. *The Journal of John Winthrop, 1630-1649*. Abridged edition. Edited by Richard S. Dunn and Laetitia Yeandle. Cambridge, Mass.: Belknap Press of Harvard University, 1996.

Michael Burgan is a freelance writer of books for children and adults. A history graduate of the University of Connecticut, he has written more than 90 fiction and nonfiction children's books. For adult audiences, he has written news articles, essays, and plays. Michael Burgan is a recipient of an Educational Press Association of America award.

Image Credits